"I AM"

KATHY LAWS

"I AM"
DAILY DEVOTIONAL

365 DAYS OF HOPE AND ENCOURAGEMENT

XULON PRESS

Xulon Press
2301 Lucien Way #415
Maitland, FL 32751
407.339.4217
www.xulonpress.com

Unless otherwise indicated, Scripture quotations taken
from the King James Version (KJV)–*public domain.*

Paperback ISBN-13: 978-1-6628-2136-3
Ebook ISBN-13: 978-1-6628-2137-0

This daily devotional offers readers statements of declaration, named "I Am" Daily Devotionals, to influence readers to realize how they were created by a loving God and how they should live each day.

Each statement is powerful in its simple word choice, while accompanied by Scripture references that relate to what is being declared. Readers will enjoy and feel encouraged by the statement of the day, while also driven to read the verse and embody it for the day. Each day reveals something new which encourages faith in God and what He has equipped us to do and become through Jesus, guided by the Holy Spirit. Readers will enjoy the variety of the content and seek to follow more closely what is being shared.

Focusing on God's word reflects who we are. "I Am" statements read daily help to develop and strengthen our inner person to withstand the struggles in everyday life experiences. When your true reflection mirrors God's word on a regular basis, you will evolve into the spiritual individual that you are called to be.

JANUARY 1

I am trusting in the Lord, and I will dwell in the land and I will be fed.

"Trust in the LORD, and do good; so shalt thou dwell in the land, and verily thou shalt be fed" (Psalms 37:3).

JANUARY 2

I am delighting in Lord and I will receive the desires of my heart.

"Delight thyself also in the LORD: and he shall give thee the desires of thine heart" (Psalms 37:4).

JANUARY 3

I am committed to the Lord and my righteousness will come forth as the light.

"Commit thy way unto the LORD; trust also in him; and he shall bring it to pass. And He shall bring forth thy righteousness as the light." (Psalms 37:5-6a).

JANUARY 4

I am resting in the Lord and waiting patiently for Him.

"Rest in the LORD, and wait patiently for him" (Psalms 37:7).

JANUARY 5

I am meek and I will have the abundance of peace.

"But the meek shall inherit the earth; and shall delight themselves in the abundance of peace" (Psalms 37:11)

JANUARY 6

I am upright and my inheritance will be eternal.

"The LORD knows the days of the upright: and their inheritance shall be forever" (Psalms 37:18).

JANUARY 7

I am righteous, I show mercy, and I give.

"The wicked borrows and pays not again:
but the righteous show mercy and gives"
(Psalms 37:21).

JANUARY 8

I am a good person, and my steps are
ordered by the Lord.

"The steps of a good man are ordered
by the LORD: and he delights in his way"
(Psalms 37:23).

JANUARY 9

I am a saint and not forsaken. I will be preserved forever.

"For the LORD loveth judgment and forsakes not his saints; they are preserved for ever: but the seed of the wicked shall be cut off" (Psalms 37:28).

JANUARY 10

I am strengthened in the time of trouble.

"But the salvation of the righteous is of the LORD: he is their strength in the time of trouble" (Psalms 37:39).

JANUARY 11

I am hopeful in the Lord and He hears my prayers.

"For in thee, O LORD, do I hope: thou wilt hear, O Lord my God" (Psalms 38:15).

JANUARY 12

I am of good courage and my heart is strengthened by the Lord as I wait on Him.

"Wait on the LORD: be of good courage, and he shall strengthen thine heart: wait, I say, on the LORD" (Psalms 27:14).

JANUARY 13

I am taught of the Lord and lead in a plain path.

"Teach me thy way, O LORD, and lead me in a plain path, because of mine enemies" (Psalms 27:11).

JANUARY 14

I am set up upon a rock when trouble comes my way.

"For in the time of trouble he shall hide me in his pavilion: in the secret of his tabernacle shall he hide me; he shall set me up upon a rock" (Psalms 27:5).

JANUARY 15

I am not afraid because the Lord is the strength of my life.

"The LORD is my light and my salvation; whom shall I fear? the LORD is the strength of my life; of whom shall I be afraid?" (Psalms 27:1).

JANUARY 16

I am confident even when war rises against me.

"Though a host should encamp against me, my heart shall not fear: though war should rise against me, in this will I be confident" (Psalms 27:3).

JANUARY 17

I am desiring to dwell in the house of the Lord all the days of my life.

Psalms 27:4 "One thing have I desired of the LORD, that will I seek after; that I may dwell in the house of the LORD all the days of my life, to behold the beauty of the LORD, and to enquire in his temple" (Psalms 27:4).

JANUARY 18

I am walking in God's truth.

"For thy lovingkindness is before mine eyes: and I have walked in thy truth" (Psalms 26:3).

JANUARY 19

I am the voice of thanksgiving and I will tell of God's wonderful works.

"That I may publish with the voice of thanksgiving and tell of all thy wondrous works" (Psalms 26:7).

JANUARY 20

I am walking in my integrity.

"But as for me, I will walk in mine integrity: redeem me, and be merciful unto me" (Psalms 26:11).

JANUARY 21

I am standing in an even place and I will bless the Lord.

"My foot stands in an even place: in the congregations will I bless the LORD" (Psalms 26:12).

JANUARY 22

I am meek, guided and taught of the Lord.

"The meek will he guides in judgment: and the meek will he teaches his way" (Psalms 25:9).

JANUARY 23

I am fearful of the Lord and taught the way
that He chooses.

"What man is he that fears the LORD?
him shall he teach in the way that he shall
choose" (Psalms 25:12).

JANUARY 24

I am looking always toward the Lord.

"Mine eyes are ever toward the LORD;
for he shall pluck my feet out of the net"
(Psalms 25:15).

JANUARY 25

I am in the paths of righteousness.

"He restoreth my soul: he leadeth me in the paths of righteousness for his name's sake" (Psalms 23:3).

JANUARY 26

I am in the house of the Lord

"Surely goodness and mercy shall follow me all the days of my life: and I will dwell in the house of the LORD forever" (Psalms 23:6).

JANUARY 27

I am anointed with oil and my cup runs over.

"Thou preparest a table before me in the presence of mine enemies: thou anoint my head with oil; my cup runs over" (Psalms 23:5).

JANUARY 28

I am blessed because I keep God's testimonies.

"Blessed are they that keep his testimonies, and that seek him with the whole heart" (Psalms 119:2).

JANUARY 29

I am rejoicing always.

"Rejoice in the Lord always: and again, I
say, Rejoice" (Philippians 4:4).

JANUARY 30

I am a meditator of God's word.

"I will meditate in thy precepts and have
respect unto thy ways" (Psalms 119:15).

I am like a tree planted by the rivers of water.

"And he shall be like a tree planted by the rivers of water, that bringeth forth his fruit in his season; his leaf also shall not wither; and whatsoever he doeth shall prosper" (Psalms 1:3).

FEBRUARY 1

I am very fruitful and whatever I do prospers.

"And he shall be like a tree planted by the rivers of water, that bringeth forth his fruit in his season; his leaf also shall not wither; and whatsoever he doeth shall prosper" (Psalms 1:3).

FEBRUARY 2

I am sustained by the Lord.

"I laid me down and slept; I awaked; for the LORD sustained me" (Psalms 3:5).

FEBRUARY 3

I am saved by the Lord.

"Arise, O LORD; save me, O my God: for thou hast smitten all mine enemies upon the cheek bone; thou hast broken the teeth of the ungodly" (Psalms 3:7).

FEBRUARY 4

I am your people, and your blessings are upon me.

"Salvation belongs to the LORD: thy blessing is upon thy people. Selah" (Psalms 3:8).

FEBRUARY 5

I am set apart because of my godliness.

"But know that the LORD hath set apart
him that is godly for himself: the LORD will
hear when I call unto him" (Psalms 4:3).

FEBRUARY 6

I am a prayer warrior. The Lord hears me.

"My voice shalt thou hear in the morning,
O LORD; in the morning will I direct my
prayer unto thee and will look up" (Psalms
5:3).

FEBRUARY 7

I am joyful in the Lord and I put my trust in Him.

"But let all those that put their trust in thee rejoice let them ever shout for joy, because thou defend them: let them also that love thy name be joyful in thee" (Psalms 5:11).

FEBRUARY 8

I am favored and covered with a shield.

"For thou, LORD, wilt bless the righteous; with favor wilt thou compass him as with a shield" (Psalms 5:12).

FEBRUARY 9

I am upright in heart and saved.

"My defense is of God, which saves the upright in heart" (Psalms 7:10).

FEBRUARY 10

I am mindful of the Lord.

"What is man, that thou art mindful of him? and the son of man, that thou visit him? (Psalms 8:4).

FEBRUARY 11

I am crowned with glory and honor.

"For thou hast made him a little lower than the angels, and hast crowned him with glory and honor" (Psalms 8:5).

FEBRUARY 12

I am dominant over the works of God's hands and all is under my feet.

"Thou made him to have dominion over the works of thy hands; thou hast put all things under his feet" (Psalms 8:6).

FEBRUARY 13

I am a praise worshipper.

"I will praise thee, O LORD, with my whole heart; I will shew forth all thy marvelous works" (Psalms 9:1).

FEBRUARY 14

I am willing and obedient and will eat the good of the land.

"If ye be willing and obedient, ye shall eat the good of the land" (Isaiah 1:19).

FEBRUARY 15

I am preserved in discretion and understanding.

"Discretion shall preserve thee; understanding shall keep thee" (Proverbs 2:11).

FEBRUARY 16

I am given wisdom from the Lord.

"For the LORD giveth wisdom: out of his mouth cometh knowledge and understanding" (Proverbs 2:6).

FEBRUARY 17

I am favored by God and man.

"So shalt thou find favor and good understanding in the sight of God and man" (Proverbs 3:4).

FEBRUARY 18

I am loved and was chosen by God even before the world was made.

"According as he hath chosen us in him before the foundation of the world, that we should be holy and without blame before him in love" (Ephesians 1:4).

FEBRUARY 19

I am loved and delighted of the Lord and He corrects me.

"For whom the LORD loveth he corrects; even as a father the son in whom he delights" (Proverbs 3:12).

FEBRUARY 20

I am finding wisdom and getting understanding. This makes me happy.

"Happy is the man that finds wisdom, and the man that gets understanding" (Proverbs 3:13).

FEBRUARY 21

I am confident in the Lord.

"For the LORD shall be thy confidence
and shall keep thy foot from being taken"
(Proverbs 3:26).

FEBRUARY 22

I am just and my path is as the shining
light.

"But the path of the just is as the shining
light, that shineth more and more unto the
perfect day" (Proverbs 4:18).

FEBRUARY 23

I am diligent in my heart; out of it flow the issues of life.

"Keep thy heart with all diligence; for out of it are the issues of life" (Proverbs 4:23).

FEBRUARY 24

I am a new creature in Christ.

"Therefore, if any man be in Christ, he is a new creature: old things are passed away; behold, all things are become new" (2 Corinthians 5:17).

FEBRUARY 25

I am reconciled to God by Christ Jesus.

"And all things are of God, who hath reconciled us to himself by Jesus Christ, and hath given to us the ministry of reconciliation" (2 Corinthians 5:18).

FEBRUARY 26

I am an ambassador for Christ.

"Now then we are ambassadors for Christ, as though God did beseech you by us: we pray you in Christ's stead, be ye reconciled to God" (2 Corinthians 5:20).

FEBRUARY 27

I am the righteousness of God in Christ Jesus.

"For he hath made him to be sin for us, who knew no sin; that we might be made the righteousness of God in him (2 Corinthians 5:21).

FEBRUARY 28

I am eternal in the heavens.

"For we know that if our earthly house of this tabernacle were dissolved, we have a building of God, a house not made with hands, eternal in the heavens" (2 Corinthians 5:1).

MARCH 1

I am walking by faith and not by sight.

"For we walk by faith and not by sight" (2 Corinthians 5:7).

MARCH 2

I am kind and compassionate to others and forgiving.

"Get rid of all bitterness, rage and anger, brawling and slander, along with every form of malice. Be kind and compassionate to one another, forgiving each other, just as in Christ God forgave you" (Ephesians 4:31-32).

MARCH 3

I am forgiven because I confess my sins
and God is faithful and just to forgive me.

"If we confess our sins, he is faithful and
just and will forgive us our sins and purify
us from all unrighteousness" (1 John 1:9).

MARCH 4

I am forgiven by my Heavenly Father if I
forgive others.

"For if you forgive other people when they
sin against you, your heavenly Father will
also forgive you. But if you do not forgive
others their sins, your Father will not
forgive your sins" (Matthew 6:14-15).

MARCH 5

I am strong in the Lord and in the power of His might.

"Finally, be strong in the Lord and in his mighty power" (Ephesians 6:10).

MARCH 6

I am seated in heavenly places in Christ Jesus.

"And hath raised us up together, and made us sit together in heavenly places in Christ Jesus" (Ephesians 2:6).

MARCH 7

I am letting my light shine before all men; they see my good works that God performs through me.

"Let your light so shine before men, that they may see your good works, and glorify your Father which is in heaven" (Matthew 5:16).

MARCH 8

I am saved by God's great grace.

"For by grace are ye saved through faith; and that not of yourselves: it is the gift of God" (Ephesians 2:8).

MARCH 9

I am a born-again believer.

"You should not be surprised at my saying, 'You must be born again" (John 3:7).

MARCH 10

I am asking and I will receive exceedingly, abundantly above what I ask or think.

"Now unto him that is able to do exceedingly, abundantly above all that we ask or think, according to the power that works in us" (Ephesians 3:20).

MARCH 11

I am the apple of the Father's eye and hidden in the shadow of His wings.

"Keep me as the apple of your eye; hide me in the shadow of your wings" (Psalm 17:8).

MARCH 12

I am the light of the world.

"Ye are the light of the world" (Matthew 5:14a).

MARCH 13

I am a city that is set on a hill and can't be hid.

"A city that is set on a hill cannot be hid" (Matthew 5:14b).

MARCH 14

I am the salt of the earth.

"Ye are the salt of the earth: but if the salt has lost his savour, wherewith shall it be salted? it is thenceforth good for nothing, but to be cast out, and to be trodden under foot of men" (Matthew 5:13).

MARCH 15

I am born of incorruptible seed through the word of God.

"For you have been born again, not of perishable seed, but of imperishable, through the living and enduring word of God" (1 Peter 1:23).

MARCH 16

I am part of a royal priesthood, a chosen generation, a holy nation.

"But you are a chosen people, a royal priesthood, a holy nation, God's special possession, that you may declare the praises of him who called you out of darkness into his wonderful light" (1 Peter 2:9).

MARCH 17

I am prospering and in good health.

"Beloved, I wish above all things that thou mayest prosper and be in health, even as thy soul prospers" (3 John 1:2).

MARCH 18

I am blessed when I come in.

"Blessed shalt thou be when thou come in, and blessed shalt thou be when thou go out" (Deuteronomy 28:6).

MARCH 19

I am Abraham's seed according to the promise.

"And if ye be Christ's, then are ye Abraham's seed, and heirs according to the promise" (Galatians 3:29).

MARCH 20

I am the head and not the tail.

"And the LORD shall make thee the head, and not the tail; and thou shalt be above only, and thou shalt not be beneath; if that thou hearken unto the commandments of the LORD thy God, which I command thee this day, to observe and to do them" (Deuteronomy 28:13).

MARCH 21

I am above and not beneath.

"And the Lord shall make thee the head, and not the tail; and thou shalt be above only, and thou shalt not be beneath; if that thou hearken unto the commandments of the Lord thy God, which I command thee this day, to observe and to do them" (Deuteronomy 28:13).

MARCH 22

I am increasing more and more, me and my children.

"The Lord shall increase you more and more, you and your children" (Psalms 115:14).

MARCH 23

I am blessed when I go out.

"Blessed shalt thou be when thou come in, and blessed shalt thou be when thou go out" (Deuteronomy 28:6).

MARCH 24

I am a world overcomer.

"Who is He that overcomes the world, but he that believeth that Jesus is the Son of God?" (1 John 5:5).

MARCH 25

I am keeping your precepts with my whole heart.

"The proud have forged a lie against me: but I will keep thy precepts with my whole heart" (Psalms 119:16).

MARCH 26

I am baptized with the Holy Ghost and fire.

"I indeed baptize you with water unto repentance. but he that cometh after me is mightier than I, whose shoes I am not worthy to bear he shall baptize you with the Holy Ghost, and with fire" (Matthew 3:11).

MARCH 27

I am in love with the brethren.

"We know that we have passed from death unto life, because we love the brethren. He that loveth not his brother abides in death" (1 John 3:14).

MARCH 28

I am a follower of Jesus Christ.

"And he (Jesus) saith unto them, follow me, and I will make you fishers of men" (Matthew 4:19).

MARCH 29

I am a disciple of Christ.

"Then said Jesus to those Jews which believed on him, if ye continue in my word, then are ye my disciples indeed" (John 8:31).

MARCH 30

I am devoted to prayer and the ministry of the word.

"But we will devote ourselves to prayer and to the ministry of the word" (Acts 6:4).

I am set apart for the glory of God.

"But know that the LORD hath set apart him that is godly for himself: the LORD will hear when I call unto him" (Psalms 4:3).

APRIL 1

I am healed by the stripes of Jesus.

"The chastisement for our peace was upon
Him, and by His stripes we are healed"
(Isaiah 53:5).

APRIL 2

I am encamped about by angels and they
deliver me.

"The angel of the LORD encamps round
about them that fear him and delivers
them" (Psalms 34:7).

APRIL 3

I am filled with the Holy Spirit.

"And when they had prayed, the place was shaken wherein they were gathered together; and they were all filled with the Holy Spirit, and they spoke the word of God with boldness" (Acts 4:31).

APRIL 4

I am celebrating the resurrection of Jesus Christ.

"Jesus rose from the dead early on the first day of the week. He appeared first to Mary Magdalene. He had driven seven demons out of her. She went and told those who had been with him. She found them crying. They were very sad. They heard that Jesus was alive and that she had seen him. But they did not believe it" (Mark 16:9-11).

APRIL 5

I am hiding your word in my heart so I will not sin.

"Thy word have I hid in mine heart, that I might not sin against thee" (Psalms 119:11).

APRIL 6

I am a sojourner on the earth. Heaven is my home.

"A sojourner I am on earth, Hide not from me Thy commands" (Psalms 119:19).

APRIL 7

I am blameless and harmless as the son/
daughter of God.

"That ye may be blameless and harmless,
the sons of God, without rebuke, in the
midst of a crooked and perverse nation,
among whom ye shine as lights in the
world" (Philippians 2:15).

APRIL 8

I am protected in the full armor of God.

"Put on the whole armor of God, that ye
may be able to stand against the wiles of
the devil" (Ephesians 6:11).

APRIL 9

I am God's workmanship, created in Christ for good works.

"For we are his workmanship, created in Christ Jesus unto good works, which God hath before ordained that we should walk in them" (Ephesians 2:10).

APRIL 10

I am a member of the body of Christ.

"Now ye are the body of Christ, and members in particular" (1 Corinthians 12:27).

APRIL 11

I am united to the Lord and am one spirit with Him.

1 Corinthians 6:17 "But he that is joined unto the Lord is one spirit" (1 Corinthians 6:17).

APRIL 12

I am the temple of the Holy Spirit.

"Know ye not that ye are the temple of God, and that the Spirit of God dwelleth in you?" (1 Corinthians 3:16).

APRIL 13

I am a friend of Christ.

"Henceforth I call you not servants; for the
servant knows not what his lord doeth:
but I have called you friends; for all things
that I have heard of my Father I have made
known unto you" (John 15:15).

APRIL 14

I am a slave of righteousness.

"Being then made free from sin, ye
became the servants of righteousness"
(Romans 6:18).

APRIL 15

I am a servant to God.

"But now being made free from sin,
and become servants to God, ye have
your fruit unto holiness, and the end
everlasting life" (Romans 6:22).

APRIL 16

I am chosen and ordained by Christ to
bear fruit.

"Ye have not chosen me, but I have chosen
you, and ordained you, that ye should go
and bring forth fruit, and that your fruit
should remain that whatsoever ye shall
ask of the Father in my name, he may give
it you" (John 15:16).

APRIL 17

I am a prisoner of Christ.

"I therefore, the prisoner of the Lord,
beseech you that ye walk worthy of
the vocation wherewith ye are called"
(Ephesians 4:1).

APRIL 18

I am righteous and holy.

"And that ye put on the new man, which
after God is created in righteousness and
true holiness" (Ephesians 4:24).

APRIL 19

I am hidden with Christ in God.

"For ye are dead, and your life is hid with Christ in God" (Colossians 3:3).

APRIL 20

I am silent before the Lord.

"Be silent, O all flesh, before the LORD: for he is raised up out of his holy habitation" (Zechariah 2:13).

APRIL 21

I am thinking on the good reports of God.

"Finally, brethren, whatsoever things
are true, whatsoever things are honest,
whatsoever things are just, whatsoever
things are pure, whatsoever things are
lovely, whatsoever things are of good
report; if there be any virtue, and if there
be any praise, think on these things"
(Philippians 4:8).

APRIL 22

I am part of the true vine and I will bring
forth more fruit.

"I am the true vine, and my Father is the
husbandman. Every branch in me that
bears not fruit he taketh away: and every
branch that bears fruit, he purges it, that it
may bring forth more fruit" (John 15:1-2).

I am filled with the divine nature of Christ and escape the corruption that is in the world through lust.

"By which have been given to us exceedingly great and precious promises, that through these you may be partakers of the divine nature, having escaped the corruption that is in the world through lust" (2 Peter 1:4).

I am an expression of the life of Christ.

"When Christ, who is our life, shall appear, then shall ye also appear with him in glory" (Colossians 3:4).

APRIL 25

I am chosen of God, holy and dearly loved.

"Therefore, as God's chosen people,
holy and dearly loved, clothe yourselves
with compassion, kindness, humility,
gentleness and patience" (Colossians
3:12).

APRIL 26

I am a child of light.

"You are all children of the light and
children of the day. We do not belong to
the night or to the darkness"
(1 Thessalonians 5:5).

APRIL 27

I am a partaker of a heavenly calling.

"Therefore, holy brothers and sisters, who share in the heavenly calling, fix your thoughts on Jesus, whom we acknowledge as our apostle and high priest" (Hebrews 3:1).

APRIL 28

I am more than a conqueror through Christ.

"No, in all these things we are more than conquerors through him who loved us" (Romans 8:37).

APRIL 29

I am a partaker with Christ and share in His life.

"We have come to share in Christ, if indeed we hold our original conviction firmly to the very end" (Hebrews 3:14).

APRIL 30

I am buried with Him in baptism and risen with Him through my faith of the operation of God.

"Buried with him in baptism, wherein also ye are risen with *him* through the faith of the operation of God, who hath raised him from the dead" (Colossians 2:12).

MAY 1

I am one of God's living stones, being built up in Christ as a spiritual house.

"You also, like living stones, are being built into a spiritual house to be a holy priesthood, offering spiritual sacrifices acceptable to God through Jesus Christ" (1 Peter 2:5).

MAY 2

I am a peculiar people.

"But ye are a chosen generation, a royal priesthood, a holy nation, a peculiar people; that ye should shew forth the praises of him who hath called you out of darkness into his marvelous light" (1 Peter 2:9).

MAY 3

I am sober and vigilant because of the adversary.

"Be sober, be vigilant; because your adversary the devil, as a roaring lion, walketh about, seeking whom he may devour" (1 Peter 5:8).

MAY 4

I am born again by the Spirit of God.

"Jesus answered, Verily, verily, I say unto thee, except a man be born of water and of the Spirit, he cannot enter the kingdom of God" (John 3:5).

MAY 5

I am an alien and stranger to this world.

"Dearly beloved, I beseech you as strangers and pilgrims, abstain from fleshly lusts, which war against the soul" (1 Peter 2:11).

MAY 6

I am a child of God who always triumphs in Christ and releases His fragrance in every place.

"Now thanks be unto God, which always causes us to triumph in Christ, and makes manifest the savor of his knowledge by us in every place" (2 Corinthians 2:14).

MAY 7

I am giving and it will come back to me.

"Give, and it shall be given unto you; good measure, pressed down, and shaken together, and running over, shall men give into your bosom" (Luke 6:38).

MAY 8

I am saved by grace.

"For by grace are ye saved through faith; and that not of yourselves: it is the gift of God" (Ephesians 2:8).

MAY 9

I am a recipient of every spiritual blessing in the heavenly places in Christ.

"Blessed be the God and Father of our Lord Jesus Christ, who hath blessed us with all spiritual blessings in heavenly places in Christ" (Ephesians 1:3).

MAY 10

I am redeemed by the blood of the Lamb.

"...and hast redeemed us to God by thy blood out of every kindred, and tongue, and people, and nation" (Revelation 5:9b).

MAY 11

I am part of the bride of Christ and am
making myself ready for Him.

"For the marriage of the Lamb is come,
and his wife hath made herself ready"
(Revelation 19:7b).

MAY 12

I am a true worshipper who worships the
Father in spirit and in truth.

"God is a Spirit: and they that worship him
must worship him in spirit and in truth"
(John 4:24).

MAY 13

I am giving in secret and the Lord shall reward me openly.

"That thine alms may be in secret: and thy Father which sees in secret himself shall reward thee openly" (Matthew 6:4).

MAY 14

I am blessed and am called to be a blessing.

"And I will make of thee a great nation, and I will bless thee, and make thy name great; and thou shalt be a blessing" (Genesis 12:2)

MAY 15

I am praying in the secret place and He
rewards me openly.

"But thou, when thou pray, enter thy closet,
and when thou hast shut thy door, pray
to thy Father which is in secret; and thy
Father which sees in secret shall reward
thee openly" (Matthew 6:6).

MAY 16

I am blessed with comfort when I mourn.

"Blessed are they that mourn: for they
shall be comforted" (Matthew 5:4).

MAY 17

I am always filled with a satisfied heart because I hunger and thirst for righteousness.

"Blessed are they which do hunger and thirst after righteousness: for they shall be filled" (Matthew 5:6).

MAY 18

I am blessed with mercy because I show mercy to others.

"Blessed are the merciful: for they shall obtain mercy" (Matthew 5:7).

MAY 19

I am blessed with visions and dreams from God because I am pure in spirit.

"Blessed are the pure in heart: for they shall see God" (Matthew 5:8).

MAY 20

I am called a son/daughter of God because I am a peacemaker.

"Blessed are the peacemakers: for they shall be called the children of God" (Matthew 5:9).

MAY 21

I am blessed because I hear the Lord's Word and act on it.

"But he said, yea rather, blessed are they that hear the word of God, and keep it" (Luke 11:28).

MAY 22

I am a doer of the Word and not a hearer only.

"But be ye doers of the word, and not hearers only, deceiving your own selves" (James 1:22).

MAY 23

I am blessed with heavenly and eternal reward.

"But lay up for yourselves treasures in heaven, where neither moth nor rust doth corrupt, and where thieves do not break through nor steal" (Matthew 6:20)

MAY 24

I am granted everything that pertains to life and to godliness.

"According as his divine power hath given unto us all things that pertain unto life and godliness, through the knowledge of him that hath called us to glory and virtue" (2 Peter 1:3)

MAY 25

I am truly blessed in all things for my
Father in heaven has chosen gladly to give
me the Kingdom.

"Fear not, little flock; for it is your Father's
good pleasure to give you the kingdom"
(Luke 12:32).

MAY 26

I am understanding the Word of God and
bringing forth good fruit and deeds.

"But he that received seed into the good
ground is he that heareth the word, and
understand it, which also bear fruit, and
bringeth forth, some a hundredfold, some
sixty, some thirty" (Matthew 13:23).

MAY 27

I am delivered from temptation and evil.

"And lead us not into temptation but
deliver us from evil: For thine is the
kingdom, and the power, and the glory,
forever. Amen" (Matthew 6:13).

MAY 28

I am receiving seed, the word of God, into
good ground, which is my heart. My heart
is good.

"But he that received seed into the good
ground is he that heareth the word, and
understand it, which also bear fruit, and
bringeth forth, some a hundredfold, some
sixty, some thirty" (Matthew 13:23).

MAY 29

I am hearing the word of the kingdom and it converts and changes me.

"Lest at any time they should see with their eyes and hear with their ears, and should understand with their heart, and should be converted, and I should heal them" (Matthew 13:15b).

MAY 30

I am granted the keys of the kingdom, and whatever I bind on earth is bound in heaven. Whatever I loose on earth has been loosed in heaven.

"And I will give unto thee the keys of the kingdom of heaven: and whatsoever thou shalt bind on earth shall be bound in heaven: and whatsoever thou shalt loose on earth shall be loosed in heaven" (Matthew 16:19).

MAY 31

I am laying my treasure up in heaven.

"But lay up for yourselves treasures in heaven, where neither moth nor rust doth corrupt, and where thieves do not break through nor steal" (Matthew 6:20).

JUNE 1

I am clothed of the Lord God, I will not worry.

"Wherefore, if God so clothe the grass of the field, which today is, and tomorrow is cast into the oven, shall he not much more clothe you, O ye of little faith?" (Matthew 6:30).

JUNE 2

I am not under guilt or condemnation.

"There is therefore now no condemnation to them which are in Christ Jesus, who walk not after the flesh, but after the Spirit" (Romans 8:1).

JUNE 3

I am an overcomer because of the blood
of Jesus and because of the word of my
testimony.

"And they overcame him by the blood
of the Lamb, and by the word of their
testimony; and they loved not their lives
unto the death" (Revelation 12:11).

JUNE 4

I am accepted in the Beloved.

"To the praise of the glory of his grace,
wherein he hath made us accepted in the
beloved" (Ephesians 1:6).

JUNE 5

I am not intimidated by the enemy's lies. He is defeated.

"When he speaks a lie, he speaks of his own: for he is a liar, and the father of it" (John 8:44b).

JUNE 6

I am surrounded with angelic protection.

"The angel of the LORD encamps round about them that fear him, and delivers them" (Psalms 34:7).

JUNE 7

I am saved of all my troubles.

"This poor man cried, and the LORD heard him, and saved him out of all his troubles" (Psalms 34:6).

JUNE 8

I am humble and will be exalted.

"And whosoever shall exalt himself shall be abased; and he that shall humble himself shall be exalted" (Matthew 23:12).

JUNE 9

I am set free because I know the truth.

John 8:32 "And ye shall know the truth, and the truth shall make you free" (John 8:32).

JUNE 10

I am free indeed because the son has set me free.

"If the Son therefore shall make you free, ye shall be free indeed" (John 8:36).

JUNE 11

I am beholding the glory of the Lord and being changed into the image of Christ from glory to glory.

"But we all, with open face beholding as in a glass the glory of the Lord, are changed into the same image from glory to glory, even as by the Spirit of the Lord" (2 Corinthians 3:18).

JUNE 12

I am elect and shall long enjoy the work of my hands.

"They shall not build, and another inhabit; they shall not plant, and another eat: for as the days of a tree are the days of my people, and mine elect shall long enjoy the work of their hands" (Isaiah 65:22).

JUNE 13

I am calling on the Lord and He hears and answers me speedily.

"And it shall come to pass, that before they call, I will answer; and while they are yet speaking, I will hear" (Isaiah 65:24).

JUNE 14

I am delivered from the power of darkness.

"Who hath delivered us from the power of darkness, and hath translated us into the kingdom of his dear Son" (Colossians 1:13).

JUNE 15

I am translated into the kingdom of His dear Son.

"Who hath delivered us from the power of darkness, and hath translated us into the kingdom of his dear Son" (Colossians 1:13).

JUNE 16

I am hidden in the secret place of the Most High.

"He that dwelleth in the secret place of the most High, shall abide under the shadow of the Almighty" (Psalms 91:1).

JUNE 17

I am defensively clad with the armor of God.

"Put on the whole armor of God, that ye may be able to stand against the wiles of the devil" (Ephesians 6:11).

JUNE 18

I am offensively equipped with the sword of the Spirit, which is the Word of God.

"And take the helmet of salvation, and the sword of the Spirit, which is the word of God" (Ephesians 6:17).

JUNE 19

I am protected by angels.

"For he shall give his angels charge over thee, to keep thee in all thy ways" (Psalms 91:11).

JUNE 20

I am blessed with national prominence and set on high because I do as the Lord commands.

"And it shall come to pass, if thou shalt hearken diligently unto the voice of the LORD thy God, to observe and to do all his commandments which I command thee this day, that the LORD thy God will set thee on high above all nations of the earth" (Deuteronomy 28:1).

JUNE 21

I am blessed in the city.

"Blessed shalt thou be in the city"
(Deuteronomy 28:3a).

JUNE 22

I am blessed in the field.

"And blessed shalt thou be in the field"
(Deuteronomy 28:3b).

JUNE 23

I am blessed to achieve fruitfulness in all areas.

"Blessed shall be the fruit of thy body, and the fruit of thy ground, and the fruit of thy cattle, the increase of thy kine, and the flocks of thy sheep" (Deuteronomy 28:4).

JUNE 24

I am blessed with daily provision.

"Blessed shalt thou be when thou come in, and blessed shalt thou be when thou go out" (Deuteronomy 28:6).

JUNE 25

I am blessed in all that my hand is put to.

Deuteronomy 28:8 "The LORD shall command the blessing upon thee in thy storehouses, and in all that thou set thine hand unto; and he shall bless thee in the land which the LORD thy God giveth thee" (Deuteronomy 28:8).

JUNE 26

I am blessed with victory and the people shall know it.

"And all people of the earth shall see that thou art called by the name of the LORD; and they shall be afraid of thee" (Deuteronomy 28:10).

JUNE 27

I am inhabiting the house that I built in the Lord.

"And they shall build houses, and inhabit them; and they shall plant vineyards, and eat the fruit of them" (Isaiah 65:21).

JUNE 28

I am called by the name of the Lord.

"And all people of the earth shall see that thou art called by the name of the LORD; and they shall be afraid of thee" (Deuteronomy 28:10).

JUNE 29

I am fearfully and wonderfully made.

"I will praise thee; for I am fearfully and wonderfully made: marvelous are thy works; and that my soul knows right well" (Psalms 139:14).

JUNE 30

I am loving God with all my heart, soul, and mind.

"And thou shalt love the Lord thy God with all thy heart, and with all thy soul, and with all thy mind, and with all thy strength: this is the first commandment" (Mark 12:30).

JULY 1

I am sealed with the Holy Spirit of promise, which is part of my inheritance.

"In whom ye also trusted, after that ye heard the word of truth, the gospel of your salvation: in whom also after that ye believed, ye were sealed with that holy Spirit of promise, which is the earnest of our inheritance until the redemption of the purchased possession, into the praise of His glory" (Ephesians 1:13-14).

JULY 2

I am a saint in Christ Jesus.

"To all who are beloved of God in Rome, called as saints: Grace to you and peace from God our Father and the Lord Jesus Christ" (Romans 1:7).

JULY 3

I am called out of darkness into His wonderful light.

"But you are a chosen people, a royal priesthood, a holy nation, God's special possession, that you may declare the praises of him who called you out of darkness into his wonderful light" (1 Peter 2:9).

JULY 4

I am loving my neighbor as myself.

"And the second is like, namely this, thou shalt love thy neighbor as thyself. There is none other commandment greater than these" (Mark 12:31).

JULY 5

I am a casting my burdens on the Lord.

"Cast thy burden upon the Lord, and he shall sustain thee: he shall never suffer the righteous to be moved" (Psalms 55:22).

JULY 6

I am calling on God and He shall save me.

"As for me, I will call upon God; and the Lord shall save me" (Psalms 55:16).

JULY 7

I am prosperous and in health as my soul prospers.

"Beloved, I wish above all things that thou mayest prosper and be in health, even as thy soul prospers" (3 John 1:2).

JULY 8

I am perfected in Christ Jesus.

"Whom we preach, warning every man, and teaching every man in all wisdom; that we may present every man perfect in Christ Jesus" (Colossians 1:28).

JULY 9

I am crucified with Christ.

"I am crucified with Christ: nevertheless, I live; yet not I, but Christ lives in me: and the life which I now live in the flesh I live by the faith of the Son of God, who loved me, and gave himself for me" (Galatians 2:20).

JULY 10

I am laboring for the Lord and my labor is not in vain.

"They shall not labor in vain, nor bring forth for trouble; for they are the seed of the blessed of the LORD, and their offspring with them" (Isaiah 65:23).

JULY 11

I am blessed to have heard the gospel and seen the things that I have seen of God.

"For verily I say unto you, that many prophets and righteous men have desired to see those things which ye see and have not seen them; and to hear those things which ye hear and have not heard them" (Matthew 13:17).

JULY 12

I am praying evening, morning and noon and my prayers are heard by God.

"Evening, and morning, and at noon, will I pray, and cry aloud: and he shall hear my voice" (Psalms 55:17).

JULY 13

I am sanctified in Christ Jesus.

"To the church of God, which is at Corinth, to those who have been sanctified in Christ Jesus, saints by calling, with all who in every place call on the name of our Lord Jesus Christ, their Lord and ours" (1 Corinthians 1:2).

JULY 14

I am justified freely by His grace.

"Being justified freely by His grace through the redemption that is in Christ Jesus" (Romans 3:24).

JULY 15

I am meek and I have salvation.

"For the LORD taketh pleasure in his
people: he will beautify the meek with
salvation" (Psalms 149:4).

JULY 16

I am taught of the Lord's statutes.

"Teach me, O LORD, the way of thy
statutes; and I shall keep it unto the end"
(Psalms 119:33).

JULY 17

I am observant of the law with my whole heart.

"Give me understanding, and I shall keep thy law; yea, I shall observe it with my whole heart" (Psalms 119:34).

JULY 18

I am quickened in the Lord's way.

"Turn away mine eyes from beholding vanity; and quicken thou me in thy way" (Psalms 119:37).

JULY 19

I am devoted to the Lord's fear.

"Stablish thy word unto thy servant, who is devoted to thy fear" (Psalms 119:38).

JULY 20

I am trusting in God's Word.

"So shall I have wherewith to answer him that reproaches me: for I trust in thy word" (Psalms 119:42).

JULY 21

I am walking in liberty.

"And I will walk at liberty: for I seek thy precepts" (Psalms 119:45).

JULY 22

I am meditating in His statutes.

"My hands also will I lift up unto thy commandments, which I have loved; and I will meditate in thy statutes" (Psalms 119:48).

JULY 23

I am reassured of God's promises.

"Reassure me of your promise, made to those who fear you" (Psalm 119:38).

JULY 24

I am renewed with your goodness.

"I long to obey your commandments! Renew my life with your goodness" (Psalm 119:40, NLT).

JULY 25

I am fulfilling the law by loving others.

"Owe no man anything, but to love one another: for he that loveth another hath fulfilled the law" (Romans 13:8).

JULY 26

I am clothed in the armor of light.

"The night is far spent, the day is at hand: let us therefore cast off the works of darkness and let us put on the armor of light" (Romans 13:12).

JULY 27

I am compassionate of others as the Lord has been compassionate of me.

"Shouldest not thou also have had compassion on thy fellow servant, even as I had pity on thee?" (Matthew 18:33).

JULY 28

I am forgiving of others as the Lord has forgiven me.

"For if ye forgive men their trespasses, your heavenly Father will also forgive you: But if ye forgive not men their trespasses, neither will your Father forgive your trespasses" (Matthew 6:14-15).

JULY 29

I am full of light, because my eye is singled on Christ Jesus.

"The light of the body is the eye: if therefore thine eye be single; thy whole body shall be full of light" (Matthew 6:22).

JULY 30

I am serving one master, the Lord, God almighty.

"No man can serve two masters: for either he will hate the one and love the other; or else he will hold to the one and despise the other. Ye cannot serve God and mammon" (Matthew 6:24).

JULY 31

I am seeking the kingdom of God first and all His righteousness is added unto me.

"But seek ye first the kingdom of God, and his righteousness; and all these things shall be added unto you" (Matthew 6:33).

AUGUST 1

I am hungering and thirsting after
righteousness and I will be filled.

"Blessed are they which do hunger and
thirst after righteousness: for they shall be
filled" (Matthew 5:6).

AUGUST 2

I am anchored in the promises of God
which were made to Abraham.

"For when God made promise to Abraham,
because he could swear by no greater, he
swore by himself" (Hebrews 6:13).

AUGUST 3

I am giving and it will come back in good measure, pressed down, shaken together, and running over.

"Give, and it shall be given unto you; good measure, pressed down, and shaken together, and running over, shall men give into your bosom. For with the same measure that ye mete withal it shall be measured to you again" (Luke 6:38).

AUGUST 4

I am covered by the blood of Jesus.

"And they shall take of the blood and strike it on the two side posts and on the upper door post of the houses, wherein they shall eat it" (Exodus 12:7).

AUGUST 5

I am entering into the most Holy place by
the blood of Jesus.

"Having therefore, brethren, boldness to
enter into the holiest by the blood of Jesus"
(Hebrews 10:19).

AUGUST 6

I am blessed while being persecuted by
others.

"Blessed are ye, when men shall revile
you, and persecute you, and shall say all
manner of evil against you falsely, for my
sake" (Matthew 5:11).

AUGUST 7

I am rejoicing and being exceedingly glad.

"Rejoice, and be exceeding glad: for great is your reward in heaven: for so persecuted they the prophets which were before you" (Matthew 5:12).

AUGUST 8

I am being perfected even as my Father in heaven is perfect.

"Be ye therefore perfect, even as your Father which is in heaven is perfect" (Matthew 5:48).

AUGUST 9

I am loving and praying for the ones who persecute me.

"But I say unto you, love your enemies, bless them that curse you, do good to them that hate you, and pray for them which despitefully use you, and persecute you" (Matthew 5:44).

AUGUST 10

I am asking, seeking and knocking and it shall be given, I will find and the door will be opened.

"Ask, and it shall be given you; seek, and ye shall find; knock, and it shall be opened unto you" (Matthew 7:7).

AUGUST 11

I am doing unto others as I would have them do unto me.

"Therefore, all things whatsoever ye would that men should do to you, do ye even so to them: for this is the law and the prophets" (Matthew 7:12).

AUGUST 12

I am entering in at the strait gate that leads to life.

"Because strait is the gate, and narrow is the way, which leadeth unto life, and few there be that find it" (Matthew 7:14).

AUGUST 13

I am a good tree that brings forth good fruit.

"A good tree cannot bring forth evil fruit, neither can a corrupt tree bring forth good fruit" (Matthew 7:18).

AUGUST 14

I am doing the will of the Father in heaven and I will enter into the kingdom of heaven.

"Not everyone that saith unto me, Lord, Lord, shall enter into the kingdom of heaven; but he that doeth the will of my Father which is in heaven" (Matthew 7:21).

AUGUST 15

I am a wise person who builds my house on a rock because I am a keeper and doer of God's Word.

"Therefore, whosoever heareth these sayings of mine, and doeth them, I will liken him unto a wise man, which built his house upon a rock" (Matthew 7:24).

AUGUST 16

I am a sheep, wise as a serpent and harmless as a dove.

"Behold, I send you forth as sheep in the midst of wolves: be ye therefore wise as serpents, and harmless as doves" (Matthew 10:16).

AUGUST 17

I am more valuable than many sparrows.

"Fear ye not therefore, ye are of more value than many sparrows" (Matthew 10:31).

AUGUST 18

I am a cross bearer who follows after Jesus.

"And he that taketh not his cross, and follow after me, is not worthy of me" (Matthew 10:38).

AUGUST 19

I am taking Jesus yoke upon me and learning of Him. His yoke is easy, and His burden is light.

"Take my yoke upon you and learn of me; for I am meek and lowly in heart: and ye shall find rest unto your souls" (Matthew 11:29).

AUGUST 20

I am a laborer that returns to Jesus and He gives me rest.

"Come unto me, all ye that labor and are heavy laden, and I will give you rest" (Matthew 11:28).

AUGUST 21

I am a believer and I have everlasting life.

"Verily, verily, I say unto you, He that heareth my word, and believeth on him that sent me, hath everlasting life, and shall not come into condemnation; but is passed from death unto life" (John 5:24).

AUGUST 22

I am victorious through our Lord Jesus Christ.

"But thanks be to God, which giveth us the victory through our Lord Jesus Christ" (1 Corinthians 15:57).

AUGUST 23

I am incorruptible.

"For this corruptible must put on incorruption, and this mortal must put on immortality" (1 Corinthians 15:53).

AUGUST 24

I am steadfast, unmovable, always abounding in the work of the Lord.

"Therefore, my beloved brethren, be ye steadfast, unmovable, always abounding in the work of the Lord, forasmuch as ye know that your labor is not in vain in the Lord" (1 Corinthians 15:58).

AUGUST 25

I am building myself up in my most holy faith.

"But ye, beloved, building up yourselves on your most holy faith, praying in the Holy Ghost" (Jude 1:20).

AUGUST 26

I am a coheir with Christ.

"And since we are his children, we are his heirs. In fact, together with Christ we are heirs of God's glory. But if we are to share his glory, we must also share his suffering" (Romans 8:17).

AUGUST 27

I am rewarded according to my righteousness and the cleanness of my hands.

"The LORD rewarded me according to my righteousness; according to the cleanness of my hands hath he recompensed me" (Psalms 18:20).

AUGUST 28

I am recompensed according to my righteousness and the cleanness of my hands.

"Therefore, hath the LORD recompensed me according to my righteousness, according to the cleanness of my hands in his eyesight" (Psalms 18:24).

AUGUST 29

I am girded with strength by God.

"It is God that girded me with strength and makes my way perfect" (Psalms 18:32).

AUGUST 30

I am lifted up over those who rise up against me.

"He delivers me from mine enemies: yea, thou lift me up above those that rise up against me: thou hast delivered me from the violent man" (Psalms 18:48).

AUGUST 31

I am of good cheer because Jesus has overcome the world.

"These things I have spoken unto you, that in me ye might have peace. In the world ye shall have tribulation: but be of good cheer; I have overcome the world" (John 16:33).

SEPTEMBER 1

I am a cheerful giver and God loves me.

"Every man according as he purposed in his heart, so let him give; not grudgingly, or of necessity: for God loveth a cheerful giver" (2 Corinthians 9:7).

SEPTEMBER 2

I am loving because the love of God has been shed in my heart by the Holy Ghost which God freely gave me.

"And hope maketh not ashamed; because the love of God is shed abroad in our hearts by the Holy Ghost which is given unto us" (Romans 5:5).

SEPTEMBER 3

I am the temple of the Holy Spirit.

"What? know ye not that your body is the temple of the Holy Ghost, which is in you, which ye have of God, and ye are not your own?" (1 Corinthians 6:19).

SEPTEMBER 4

I am given a spirit of power, love, and a sound mind.

"For God hath not given us the spirit of fear; but of power, and of love, and of a sound mind" (2 Timothy 1:7).

SEPTEMBER 5

I am equipped with strength for the battle.

"For thou hast girded me with strength
unto the battle: thou hast subdued
under me those that rose up against me"
(Psalms 18:39).

SEPTEMBER 6

I am cleansed of the Lord and free of guilt.

"How can I know all the sins lurking in my
heart?

Cleanse me from these hidden faults.
Keep your servant from deliberate sins!
Don't let them control me. Then I will be
free of guilt and innocent of great sin"
(Psalms 19:12-13).

SEPTEMBER 7

I am chastened and disciplined of the Lord.

"Thou shalt also consider in thine heart, that, as a man chastened his son, so the LORD thy God chastened thee" (Deuteronomy 8:5).

SEPTEMBER 8

I am called according to God's purpose and all things work together for my good.

"And we know that all things work together for good to them that love God, to them who are the called according to his purpose" (Romans 8:28).

SEPTEMBER 9

I am glad to boast about my weakness
so that the power of Christ can work
through me.

"Each time he said, "My grace is all you need.
My power works best in weakness." So now
I am glad to boast about my weaknesses, so
that the power of Christ can work through
me" (2 Corinthians 12:9-10).

SEPTEMBER 10

I am surrounded by a cloud of witnesses
and I run patiently in the race that's set
before me.

"Wherefore seeing we also are compassed
about with so great a cloud of witnesses,
let us lay aside every weight, and the sin
which doth so easily beset us, and let
us run with patience the race that is set
before us" (Hebrews 12:1).

SEPTEMBER 11

I am living by faith in the son of God who loves me and died for me.

"I am crucified with Christ: nevertheless, I live; yet not I, but Christ lives in me: and the life which I now live in the flesh I live by the faith of the Son of God, who loved me, and gave himself for me" (Galatians 2:20).

SEPTEMBER 12

I am walking by faith and not by sight.

"For we walk by faith, not by sight" (2 Corinthians 5:7).

SEPTEMBER 13

I am rising up in the name of Jesus.

"Then Peter said, Silver and gold have I none; but such as I have give I thee: In the name of Jesus Christ of Nazareth rise up and walk" (Acts 3:6).

SEPTEMBER 14

I am chosen to be holy and blameless before God in love.

"According as he hath chosen us in him before the foundation of the world, that we should be holy and without blame before him in love" (Ephesians 1:4).

SEPTEMBER 15

I am an adopted child in Jesus Christ.

"Having predestinated us unto the adoption of children by Jesus Christ to himself, according to the good pleasure of his will" (Ephesians 1:5).

SEPTEMBER 16

I am fathered by God, and so I cry Abba Father.

"For ye have not received the spirit of bondage again to fear; but ye have received the Spirit of adoption, whereby we cry, Abba, Father" (Romans 8:15).

SEPTEMBER 17

I am redeemed through His blood and forgiven of sins, by the riches of His grace.

"In whom we have redemption through his blood, the forgiveness of sins, according to the riches of his grace" (Ephesians 1:7).

SEPTEMBER 18

I am knowledgeable of the mystery of His will.

"Having made known unto us the mystery of his will, according to his good pleasure which he hath purposed in himself" (Ephesians 1:9).

SEPTEMBER 19

I am praying for others often.

"For God is my witness, whom I serve with my spirit in the gospel of his Son, that without ceasing I make mention of you always in my prayers" (Romans 1:9).

SEPTEMBER 20

I am enlightened to know the hope of God's calling for my life.

"The eyes of your understanding being enlightened; that ye may know what the hope of his calling is, and what the riches of the glory of his inheritance in the saints" (Ephesians 1:18).

SEPTEMBER 21

I am a believer of His exceeding greatness and mighty power.

"And what is the exceeding greatness of his power to us-ward who believe, according to the working of his mighty power" (Ephesians 1:19).

SEPTEMBER 22

I am far above all principality, and power, and might, and dominion.

"Far above all principality, and power, and might, and dominion, and every name that is named, not only in this world, but also in that which is to come" (Ephesians 1:21).

SEPTEMBER 23

I am loved by a rich, merciful God.

"But God, who is rich in mercy, for his great love wherewith he loved us" (Ephesians 2:4)

SEPTEMBER 24

I am shown the riches of God's grace towards me through Christ Jesus.

"That in the ages to come he might shew the exceeding riches of his grace in his kindness toward us through Christ Jesus" (Ephesians 2:7).

SEPTEMBER 25

I am serving my God with my spirit in the gospel.

"For God is my witness, whom I serve with my spirit in the gospel of his Son, that without ceasing I make mention of you always in my prayers" (Romans 1:9).

SEPTEMBER 26

I am brought near and close to God by the blood of Christ Jesus.

"But now in Christ Jesus ye who sometimes were far off are made nigh by the blood of Christ" (Ephesians 2:13).

SEPTEMBER 27

I am a fellow citizen with the saints and I'm in the household of God.

"Now therefore ye are no more strangers and foreigners, but fellow citizens with the saints, and of the household of God" (Ephesians 2:19).

SEPTEMBER 28

I am built upon the foundation of the apostles and prophets of God.

"And are built upon the foundation of the apostles and prophets, Jesus Christ himself being the chief corner stone" (Ephesians 2:20).

SEPTEMBER 29

I am built together for a habitation of God through the Spirit of God.

"In whom ye also are built together for a habitation of God through the Spirit" (Ephesians 2:22).

SEPTEMBER 30

I am pressing toward the mark of the high call in Christ Jesus.

"I press toward the mark for the prize of the high calling of God in Christ Jesus" (Philippians 3:14).

OCTOBER 1

I am worshiping God in the Spirit and I have no confidence in the flesh.

"For we are the circumcision, which worship God in the spirit, and rejoice in Christ Jesus, and have no confidence in the flesh" (Philippians 3:3).

OCTOBER 2

I am counting all things loss for Christ.

"Yea doubtless, and I count all things but loss for the excellency of the knowledge of Christ Jesus my Lord: for whom I have suffered the loss of all things, and do count them but dung, that I may win Christ" (Philippians 3:8).

OCTOBER 3

I am of the righteousness of God in Christ Jesus by faith.

"And be found in him, not having mine own righteousness, which is of the law, but that which is through the faith of Christ, the righteousness which is of God by faith" (Philippians 3:9).

OCTOBER 4

I am forgetting those things which are behind and reaching to the things before.

"Brethren, I count not myself to have apprehended: but this one thing I do, forgetting those things which are behind, and reaching forth unto those things which are before" (Philippians 3:13).

OCTOBER 5

I am looking for the Savior, the Lord Jesus Christ.

"For our conversation is in heaven; from whence also we look for the Savior, the Lord Jesus Christ" (Philippians 3:20).

OCTOBER 6

I am standing fast in the Lord.

"Therefore, my brethren dearly beloved and longed for, my joy and crown, so stand fast in the Lord, my dearly beloved" (Philippians 4:1).

OCTOBER 7

I am studying the Word of God to show myself approved by God so that I will not be ashamed.

"Study to shew thyself approved unto God, a workman that needeth not to be ashamed, rightly dividing the word of truth" (2 Timothy 2:15).

OCTOBER 8

I am content in the state that I am in.

"Not that I speak in respect of want for I have learned, in whatsoever state I am, therewith to be content" (Philippians 4:11).

OCTOBER 9

I am strengthened in Christ Jesus.

"I can do all things through Christ which strengthened me" (Philippians 4:13).

OCTOBER 10

I am supplied all I need in Christ Jesus.

"But my God shall supply all your need according to his riches in glory by Christ Jesus" (Philippians 4:19).

OCTOBER 11

I am walking worthy of the Lord and am
fruitful in every good work.

"That ye might walk worthy of the Lord
unto all pleasing, being fruitful in
every good work, and increasing in the
knowledge of God" (Colossians 1:10).

OCTOBER 12

I am holy and cannot be blamed in His
sight.

"In the body of his flesh through death, to
present you holy and unblameable and
unreproveable in his sight" (Colossians
1:22).

OCTOBER 13

I am a minister in Christ Jesus.

"Whereof I am made a minister, according to the dispensation of God, which is given to me for you, to fulfil the word of God" (Colossians 1:25).

OCTOBER 14

I am grounded and settled in Christ Jesus.

"If ye continue in the faith grounded and settled and be not moved away from the hope of the gospel, which ye have heard, and which was preached to every creature which is under heaven; whereof I Paul am made a minister" (Colossians 1:23).

OCTOBER 15

I am laboring and striving according to Christ working in and through me.

"Whereunto I also labor, striving according to his working, which worketh in me mightily" (Colossians 1:29).

OCTOBER 16

I am sowing good seed bountifully. I will be blessed and reap bountifully.

"But this I say, He which soweth sparingly shall reap also sparingly; and he which soweth bountifully shall reap also bountifully" (2 Corinthians 9:6).

OCTOBER 17

I am set apart for the gospel of God.

"Paul, a servant of Jesus Christ, called to be an apostle, separated unto the gospel of God" (Romans 1:1).

OCTOBER 18

I am righteous and living by faith.

"For therein is the righteousness of God revealed from faith to faith: as it is written, the just shall live by faith" (Romans 1:17).

OCTOBER 19

I am a light to the ones who are living in darkness.

"And art confident that thou thyself art a guide of the blind, a light of them which are in darkness" (Romans 2:19).

OCTOBER 20

I am justified by faith.

"Therefore, having been justified by faith, we have peace with God through our Lord Jesus Christ" (Romans 5:1).

OCTOBER 21

I am justified by His blood.

"Much more then, being now justified
by his blood, we shall be saved from the
wrath through him" (Romans 5:9).

OCTOBER 22

I am reconciled to God by the death of His
Son, Jesus Christ.

"For if, when we were enemies, we were
reconciled to God by the death of his Son,
much more, being reconciled, we shall be
saved by his life" (Romans 5:10).

OCTOBER 23

I am reigning in life through Jesus Christ.

"For if by one man's offence death reigned by one; much more they which receive abundance of grace and of the gift of righteousness shall reign in life by one, Jesus Christ" (Romans 5:17).

OCTOBER 24

I am baptized into Christ Jesus

"Know ye not, that so many of us as were baptized into Jesus Christ" (Romans 6:3a).

OCTOBER 25

I am baptized with the Holy Ghost.

"I indeed have baptized you with water: but he shall baptize you with the Holy Ghost" (Mark 1:8).

OCTOBER 26

I am increasing learning and becoming a wiser person.

"A wise man will hear, and will increase learning; and a man of understanding shall attain unto wise counsels" (Proverbs 1:5).

OCTOBER 27

I am delighting in the sabbath and I shall ride on the high places of the earth.

"If thou turn away thy foot from the sabbath, from doing thy pleasure on my holy day; and call the sabbath a delight, the holy of the LORD, honorable; and shalt honor him, not doing thine own ways, nor finding thine own pleasure, nor speaking thine own words: Then shalt thou delight thyself in the LORD; and I will cause thee to ride upon the high places of the earth" (Isaiah 58:13-14a).

OCTOBER 28

I am hearkened to the Lord and I am safe.

"But whoso hearkens unto me shall dwell safely and shall be quiet from fear of evil" (Proverbs 1:33).

OCTOBER 29

I am receiving God's Word and hiding His commandments in my heart.

"My son, if thou wilt receive my words, and hide my commandments with thee; Then shalt thou understand the fear of the Lord AND find the knowledge of God" (Proverbs 2:1, 5).

OCTOBER 30

I am honoring the Lord with my substance and first fruits and so shall my barns be filled.

"Honor the Lord with thy substance, and with the first fruits of all thine increase: So, shall thy barns be filled with plenty" (Proverbs 3:9,10a).

OCTOBER 31

I am looking unto the Lord for my salvation.

"Therefore I will look to the LORD; I will wait for the God of my salvation; My God will hear me" (Micah 7:7).

NOVEMBER 1

I am walking in the name of the Lord forever and ever.

"For all people will walk everyone in the name of his god, and we will walk in the name of the LORD our God for ever and ever" (Micah 4:5).

NOVEMBER 2

I am a confessor of the truth that Jesus Is Lord.

"And that every tongue should confess that Jesus Christ is Lord, to the glory of God the Father" (Philippians 2:11).

NOVEMBER 3

I am fed in the strength of the Lord and
His majestic name.

"And he shall stand and feed in the
strength of the LORD, in the majesty of the
name of the LORD his God; and they shall
abide: for now shall he be great unto the
ends of the earth" (Micah 5:4).

NOVEMBER 4

I am justified and glorified by God.

"Moreover, whom he did predestinate,
them he also called: and whom he called,
them he also justified: and whom he
justified, them he also glorified" (Romans
8:30).

NOVEMBER 5

I am graciously given all things by God. He lavishes His love upon me.

"He who did not spare his own Son, but gave him up for us all—how will he not also, along with him, graciously give us all things?" (Romans 8:32).

NOVEMBER 6

I am convinced that I cannot be separated from the love of God.

"For I am persuaded, that neither death, nor life, nor angels, nor principalities, nor powers, nor things present, nor things to come, nor height, nor depth, nor any other creature, shall be able to separate us from the love of God, which is in Christ Jesus our Lord" (Romans 8:38).

NOVEMBER 7

I am clay, God is the potter; therefore, I am the work of God's hand.

"But now, O LORD, you *are* our Father; We *are* the clay, and You our potter; And all we *are* the work of Your hand" (Isaiah 64:8).

NOVEMBER 8

I am transformed by the renewing of my mind as I study the Word of God.

"And do not be conformed to this world, but be transformed by the renewing of your mind, that you may prove what *is* that good and acceptable and perfect will of God" (Romans 12:2).

NOVEMBER 9

I am overcoming evil with good.

"Be not overcome of evil but overcome evil with good" (Romans 12:21).

NOVEMBER 10

I am boasting in the Lord.

"Therefore, as it is written: "Let the one who boasts boast in the Lord..."
(1 Corinthians 1:31, NIV).

NOVEMBER 11

I am a co-worker in God's service.

"For we are co-workers in God's service;
you are God's field, God's building" (1
Corinthians 3:9).

NOVEMBER 12

I am laying a foundation as a wise builder.

"By the grace God has given me, I laid a
foundation as a wise builder, and someone
else is building on it. But each one should
build with care" (1 Corinthians 3:10)

NOVEMBER 13

I am delivered from all my afflictions.

"Many are the afflictions of the righteous:
but the LORD delivers him out of them all"
(Psalms 34:19).

NOVEMBER 14

I am a servant of Christ.

This, then, is how you ought to regard
us: as servants of Christ and as those
entrusted with the mysteries God has
revealed" (1 Corinthians 4:1).

NOVEMBER 15

I am of one Spirit and baptized into one body.

"For we were all baptized by one Spirit so as to form one body—whether Jews or Gentiles, slave or free—and we were all given the one Spirit to drink" (1 Corinthians 12:13).

NOVEMBER 16

I am bearing, believing, hoping, and enduring all things.

"Bearing all things, believeth all things, hopeth all things, enduring all things" (1 Corinthians 13:7).

NOVEMBER 17

I am rejoicing in the truth.

"Rejoicing not in iniquity but rejoicing in
the truth" (1 Corinthians 13:6).

NOVEMBER 18

I am delighting in the law of the Lord, and
in His law I meditate day and night.

"But whose delight is in the law of the Lord,
and who meditates on his law, day and
night" (Psalms 1:2).

NOVEMBER 19

I am sustained by the Lord.

"I laid me down and slept; I awaked; for the Lord sustained me."

NOVEMBER 20

I am walking humbly with the Lord.

"And what doth the LORD require of thee, but to do justly, and to love mercy, and to walk humbly with thy God?" (Micah 6:8b).

NOVEMBER 21

I am writing the vision that is given to me by God and making it plain.

"And the LORD answered me, and said, Write the vision, and make it plain upon tables, that he may run that read it" (Habakkuk 2:2).

NOVEMBER 22

I am a fellow citizen with God's people and a member of His household.

"Consequently, you are no longer foreigners and strangers, but fellow citizens with God's people and also members of his household" (Ephesians 2:19).

NOVEMBER 23

I am waiting on the promises of God, though they tarry, they will surely come to pass.

"Though it tarry, wait for it; because it will surely come, it will not tarry" (Habakkuk 2:3b).

NOVEMBER 24

I am renewing day by day.

"For which cause we faint not; but though our outward man perish, yet the inward man is renewed day by day" (2 Corinthians 4:16).

NOVEMBER 25

I am trusting in the Lord and He Knows it.

"The LORD *is* good, A stronghold in the day of trouble; And He knows those who trust in Him" (Nahum 1:7).

NOVEMBER 26

I am rejoiced over with joy and singing.

"The LORD thy God in the midst of thee is mighty; he will save, he will rejoice over thee with joy; he will rest in his love, he will joy over thee with singing" (Zephaniah 3:17).

NOVEMBER 27

I am resisting the enemy and he will flee.

"Resist the devil, and he will flee from you" (James 4:7b).

NOVEMBER 28

I am created in the image of God.

"So God created man in his own image, in the image of God created he him; male and female created he them" (Genesis 1:27).

I am turning to the Lord and He will turn to me.

"Therefore say thou unto them, Thus saith the LORD of hosts; Turn ye unto me, saith the LORD of hosts, and I will turn unto you, saith the LORD of hosts" (Zechariah 1:3).

I am walking in the Lord's ways.

"Thus saith the LORD of hosts; If thou wilt walk in my ways, and if thou wilt keep my charge, then thou shalt also judge my house, and shalt also keep my courts, and I will give thee places to walk among these that stand by" (Zechariah 3:7).

DECEMBER 1

I am strengthened in the Lord and will walk
in His name.

"And I will strengthen them in the LORD;
and they shall walk up and down in his
name, saith the LORD" (Zechariah 10:12).

DECEMBER 2

I am a tither and blessings are poured out
for me.

"Bring ye all the tithes into the storehouse,
that there may be meat in mine house,
and prove me now herewith, saith the
LORD of hosts, if I will not open you the
windows of heaven, and pour you out a
blessing, that there shall not be room
enough to receive it" (Malachi 3:10).

DECEMBER 3

I am compassionate towards the Lord
Jesus Christ and the saints.

"Hearing of thy love and faith, which thou
hast toward the Lord Jesus, and toward all
saints" (Philemon 1:5).

DECEMBER 4

I am abundantly satisfied and will drink of
the river of pleasures.

"They shall be abundantly satisfied
with the fatness of thy house; and thou
shalt make them drink of the river of thy
pleasures" (Psalms 36:8).

DECEMBER 5

I am bold in Christ.

"Wherefore, though I might be much
bold in Christ to enjoin thee that which is
convenient" (Philemon 1:8).

DECEMBER 6

I am Joyful in the Lord and rejoicing in His
salvation.

"And my soul shall be joyful in the LORD: it
shall rejoice in his salvation" (Psalms 35:9).

DECEMBER 7

I am delivered from the ones who are too strong for me.

"All my bones shall say, Lord, who is like unto thee, which delivers the poor from him that is too strong for him, yea, the poor and the needy from him that spoil him?" (Psalms 35:10).

DECEMBER 8

I am humbled with fasting and prayer.

"But as for me, when they were sick, my clothing was sackcloth: I humbled my soul with fasting; and my prayer returned into mine own bosom" (Psalms 35:13).

DECEMBER 9

I am vindicated and made clear of blame according to God's righteousness.

"Judge me, O LORD my God, according to thy righteousness; and let them not rejoice over me" (Psalms 35:24).

DECEMBER 10

I am glad and I continuously say "Let the Lord be magnified."

"Let them say continually, Let the LORD be magnified, which hath pleasure in the prosperity of his servant" (Psalms 35:27b).

DECEMBER 11

I am speaking of God's righteousness, all day long.

"And my tongue shall speak of thy righteousness and of thy praise all the day long" (Psalms 35:28).

DECEMBER 12

I am thirsty for God, the living God.

"My soul thirst for God, for the living God: when shall I come and appear before God?" (Psalms 42:2).

DECEMBER 13

I am continually preserved by God.

"Withhold not thou thy tender mercies
from me, O Lord: let thy lovingkindness
and thy truth continually preserve me"
(Psalms 40:11).

DECEMBER 14

I am helped by God.

"Be pleased, O Lord, to deliver me: O Lord,
make haste to help me" (Psalms 40:13).

DECEMBER 15

I am blessed because I consider the poor.

"Blessed is he that considers the poor:
the LORD will deliver him in time of trouble"
(Psalms 41:1).

DECEMBER 16

I am thought of by the Lord.

"Many, O LORD my God, are thy wonderful
works which thou hast done, and thy
thoughts which are to us-ward: they
cannot be reckoned up in order unto thee"
(Psalms 40:5).

DECEMBER 17

I am blessed because I trust in the Lord.

"Blessed is that man that makes the Lord
his trust, and respects not the proud, nor
such as turn aside to lies" (Psalms 40:4).

DECEMBER 18

I am delightful in doing God's will.

"I delight to do thy will, O my God: yea, thy
law is within my heart" (Psalms 40:8).

DECEMBER 19

I am a partaker of the heavenly calling.

"Wherefore, holy brethren, partakers of the heavenly calling, consider the Apostle and High Priest of our profession, Christ Jesus" (Hebrews 3:1).

DECEMBER 20

I am in peace because my soul has been delivered.

"He hath delivered my soul in peace from the battle that was against me: for there were many with me" (Psalms 55:18).

DECEMBER 21

I am waiting on the Lord and will mount up with wings like eagles.

"But those who wait on the LORD Shall renew *their* strength; They shall mount up with wings like eagles, They shall run and not be weary, They shall walk and not faint" (Isaiah 40:31).

DECEMBER 22

I am given authority to tread upon serpents and scorpions and over all the power of the enemy.

"Behold, I give unto you power to tread on serpents and scorpions, and over all the power of the enemy: and nothing shall by any means hurt you" (Luke 10:19).

DECEMBER 23

I am fasting and praying to the Father in heaven and He rewards me openly.

"That thou appear not unto men to fast, but unto thy Father which is in secret: and thy Father, which sees in secret, shall reward thee openly" (Matthew 6:18).

DECEMBER 24

I am established, anointed, and sealed by God in Christ Jesus, and the Spirit dwells in my heart.

"Now He who stablished us with you in Christ, and hath anointed us, is God, who hath also sealed us and given the earnest of the Spirit in our hearts" (2 Corinthians 2:21-22).

DECEMBER 25

I am praising God for the birth of my Lord and Savior Jesus Christ! He is the Prince of Peace!

"For unto us a Child is born, Unto us a Son is given; And the government will be upon His shoulder. And His name will be called Wonderful, Counselor, Mighty God, Everlasting Father, Prince of Peace" (Isaiah 9:6).

DECEMBER 26

I am redeemed and forgiven of all my sins. The debt against me has been canceled.

"In whom we have redemption through his blood, even the forgiveness of sins" (Colossians 1:14).

DECEMBER 27

I am believing in Jesus; therefore, I shall not perish. I will have everlasting life and dwell with Him forever.

"For God so loved the world, that He gave His only begotten Son, that whosoever believes in Him should not perish, but have everlasting life" (John 3:16).

DECEMBER 28

I am opening the doors of my heart so the King of Glory, the Lord strong and mighty, can come in.

"Lift up your heads, you gates; be lifted up, you ancient doors, that the King of glory may come in. Who is this King of glory? The Lord strong and mighty, the Lord mighty in battle. Lift up your heads, you gates; lift them up, you ancient doors, that the King of glory may come in" (Psalm 24:8).

DECEMBER 29

I am humble and crowned with victory.
The Lord delights in me!

"For the LORD delights in his people; he
crowns the humble with victory" (Psalm
149:4).

DECEMBER 30

I am redeemed by the Messiah from the
curse of the law.

"The Messiah redeemed us from the curse
of the Law by becoming a curse for us. For
it is written, "A curse on everyone who is
hung on a tree!" (Galatians 3:13).

DECEMBER 31

I am free from my sins by the blood that Jesus shed.

"Grace and peace to you from the one who is, who always was, and who is still to come; from the sevenfold Spirit before his throne; and from Jesus Christ. He is the faithful witness to these things, the first to rise from the dead, and the ruler of all the kings of the world. All glory to him who loves us and has freed us from our sins by shedding his blood for us. He has made us a Kingdom of priests for God his Father. All glory and power to him forever and ever! Amen" (Revelation 1:4b,5-6).

Putting God's Word in your heart about "**who you are**" gives you a strong defense against negative thoughts and allegations that are made against you. This daily devotional will have a great impact on your life. As you study, you will gain inner spiritual strength to face each new day with "**I Am**" daily devotionals.

The Most important "**I Am**" statement that a person can claim is: "**I am** believing in Jesus, therefore, I shall not perish. I will have everlasting life and dwell with Him forever."

This statement is based on John 3:16: "For God so loved the world, that He gave His only begotten Son, that whosoever believes in Him should not perish, but have everlasting life."

Implementing the Word of God in your life in the format of powerfully written "**I Am**" devotional statements is vital, especially during oppressive pandemic times that are sweeping across our nation and around the world. You will be spiritually strengthened as you read and quote "who you are" in God's eyes in your devotional times and on a regular basis.

Claiming "who you are" and the word of God is essential and imperative for living a whole, healthy, and enjoyable life!

By: Kathy Laws

CPSIA information can be obtained
at www.ICGtesting.com
Printed in the USA
LVHW022342151221
706125LV00004B/40